Ladybug~
I AM PROI
OF YOU :)

dreaming, map you'T
put action
behind
every
GOAT!

you
Autie

GOLD
MEDAL DOC
FROM GOALS TO GOAT
DR. ERIN HASSLER

You GOT THIS!
#GOAT

1

GOLD MEDAL DOC

From Goals to GOAT

Dr. Erin Hassler

Disclaimer

Some names have been changed to protect individuals' privacy.

This book does not replace the advice of individual medical consultation. Seek the advice of your personal physician prior to making any adjustments in diet, exercise or recovery plans.

The information in this book was correct at the time of publication, therefore the author does not assume any liability for loss or damage caused by errors or omissions. Every effort has been made to contact all copyright holders.

The term G.O.A.T. is an acronym. For the purposes of this book and illustration, the term will be written as GOAT, a noun. It will be used interchangeably.

E-book: ISBN: 978-1-7379410-1-9

Paperback: ISBN: 978-1-7379410-9-5

First E-book edition: September 2021

Editors: Thomasina Hassler and Mickey Hassler

Contributor: Xavier Hassler-Godfrey

Proofreader: Ashley Armstrong

Cover Art: Vanika Jordan

Layout: Content Champions - B. Joan Wilson

Cover Photographs: Photography by Amelia - Amelia Jackson

Hair Stylist: Mass Appeal by Episodes - Donita Richell Conner Bessard

Make-up Artist: JJ MUA - Ava Gilchrist

Publisher:

On The Clock Sportz Management and Entertainment

5090 Richmond Ave PMB 342

Houston, TX 77056

www.otcsportz.com

Thank you to LOVEY, my most favorite person in the entire world. Without you, I couldn't do any of the things God has enabled me to do. I am your biggest fan and enjoy being your Madre. I am excited about watching God's promises unfold in your life. Glad to know that hands down, you have my back.

To my Daddy, Mommy, my sisters and brothers, nieces, nephews, cousins, aunts, uncles, all of my friend-fams, my mentors, mentees, athletes, clients, colleagues, teachers, students, all my supporters, and even those who don't know quite how to handle me. When I win, we all win!

Every experience, good or bad, leads us closer to the truest version of ourselves. We each have the choice to run from it or embrace it. I've made my choice. What's yours?

Truth = Freedom = Power

Dr. Erin Hassler
Gold Medal Doc

TABLE OF CONTENTS

PROLOGUE

For most of my life, track and field has been there. As a child, I learned that running is freedom. It gave me the chance to let go without a care in the world. No chores, no homework, just me and my feet. Racing in the street, I couldn't be defeated. I took on every challenge, knowing that any boy or girl that came my way would lose. Throughout high school, track and field gave me confidence and exposed me to new people and opportunities. I was able to make new friends and gain a better understanding of who I was becoming.

I walked away from the sport as a freshman in college. I knew that as a student at Clark Atlanta University, there would be more to do than sports. I thought I was a decent athlete but had no understanding of how it worked at that level. College sports seemed to be far too advanced for what I could bring to the table. But God...

God knew me and what I needed far better than I did. Two years into my undergraduate experience in Atlanta, majoring in Biology, actively participating in campus and sorority life, I found myself looking for more. I tried out and earned a walk-on spot and later a scholarship on the women's track and field team. I would have never guessed that what I learned from my coach and Olympic hurdler, Pam Page in only two years, would shape my life forever.

My love for sports has contributed to my thought process and how I view life. This book allows you to step into my process of goal-setting and manifestation. It is my hope that you gain some insight into your own life and the courage to go after everything that you deserve.

GOATs don't ask if they deserve the best, they

expect the BEST because they are GOATs!

~Erin Hassler, DAT, ATC, LAT, PES, GOAT

CHAPTER 1:

Start with the GOAT in Mind

G-O-A-T

GREATEST OF ALL TIME

That is such a superlative description of an individual. It has typically been reserved for the world's most astounding athletes or entertainers. Often, they are only referred to by one name: Michael, Serena, Magic, Muhammed, Kobe, Pele, Aretha. While others by a nickname: Tiger, Flo Jo, Wilma, Pac. No matter the name, the title is the same.

GOAT

What does it take to earn that title? Just like anything worth doing, it takes hard work and dedication. We all know people who have dreams and aspirations, they work hard, and yet many never achieve them. So what are GOATs doing differently?

For starters, they plan to succeed. Having a dream is great, but dreams are abstract. They are representations of your thoughts or imagination. Dreams can give you hope. They can be dark as nightmares. Dreams can be vivid and seem as tangible. Some dreams are even palpable. They can guide your decisions, but they are not concrete. There is no action in dreaming. At least not without a plan.

Plans are laid out in goals. Merriam-Webster defines a goal as the end toward which effort is directed.[1] It is the thing toward which your energy is aimed. It is also described as the terminal point in a race.[2] Goals are active. For some people, the goal may be expressed exactly like the dream. For others, it may be just an outline of the highlights of that dream.

As a young child, I enjoyed playing in the dirt, digging worms, eating honeysuckle, playing with dump trucks and Barbie dolls. I played hard all day and even harder after school. As I daydreamed, I sometimes felt like I had experienced them before. I believe that is called déjà vu. Inquisitive and thoughtful, my brain never rested. When my parents spent time talking with me, it was with a sense of inclusion, as if my thoughts and dreams were important. In a time when children were supposed to be "seen and not heard", there were rules and expectations. However, I was allowed to at least speak up, with an occasional raised eyebrow or clearing of the throat from my mother.

For as long as I can remember, goal-setting was a part of my life. My parents both with backgrounds in education and a strong commitment to God, each other, and to ensuring that their children had no limits placed on them. As I look back, it seemed as if every decision

they made for us was intentional and had an expected
outcome.

I grew up in a very old two-story house in St.
Louis, Missouri's north side. It had a finished
basement, a big backyard with a swing set, and a
detached garage. An obviously segregated city but rich
with history and culture that helped to underline my
parents' intent, no limits. Representation mattered.
We saw people who looked like us doing great things.
From the doctor to the accountant, the plumber to the
librarian, they gave me a subliminal look at what was
possible.

On the swinging kitchen door, the kind that you
might see in a restaurant hung vertically a 22 x 28-inch
poster board. At the top was a picture of me sitting on
the kitchen floor in front of the radiator. I had on a red
and blue turtleneck sweater with my hair styled in two
ponytails, one-half unbraided. On top of my sweater, I
wore a white pillowcase with armholes. It was a

homemade Halloween costume, and I was no more than five years old.

The most important part of this poster...it was all about me. It was in my own handwriting and listed at least a dozen or more affirmations and goals. I do not remember every item but I remember how it made me feel. I felt as if there was not anything that I could not do. At that age, I am sure that I did not fully realize what I was doing, but my parents did. They were giving me the fuel for my dreams and visions to become goals, and my goals to become reality.

GOATs take the definition of goals literally. With each goal set, they envision the finish from the start. In my career as an athletic trainer and coach, I have been blessed to have seen this in some of the greatest athletes in the world. Just as in a race on the track, the runner knows the desired outcome before the race ever begins. They know that they want to cross the finish line first. They know that they want to be on that medal stand. It is the expected end.

So, if you want to be a G.O.A.T, then you start by planning to be the GOAT from the beginning. Your goals should be in alignment with that for which you aim. You may not be able to see the steps in between, but as long as you can see the end, then you are already halfway there.

CHAPTER 2:

Training/Conditioning – Trust the Process

So you have a goal. Goals without action are just dreams. Actions without order can be a bit chaotic. Goal setting should be concrete, measurable, and realistic over a period of time. Life, like sports, can be marked by cycles and phases. With each one, there are boundaries and targeted expectations.

In elite sports, a sound training and conditioning program is essential for ultimate and intended success. It helps to give some structure to the route toward the end goal. For GOATs a rigorous training and conditioning schedule is more than part of the sport, it is a way of life. Elite athletes live by the cycle, whether it be preseason, pre-competition, competition and off-season.[3] Another example would be, students and educators split the academic calendar into quarters, blocks, or semesters and always incorporate holidays and breaks. Each cycle has specific tasks associated with it.

In life, these phases may be a little bit more difficult to identify. There are peaks and valleys, highs and lows. Ideally, we would all like to have nothing but successes. However it just does not work that way. In order to move forward and progress toward your goals, you have to understand this ebb and flow.

In the quest to improve in a particular aspect of your training, the SAID principle can explain the process.[4,5] Once you have performed a task, the body normalizes that movement or technique. That means that the next time you perform that same task the quality can stagnate or be reduced. In order to overcome this deficiency, the training components must impose a demand on the body. The SAID (Specific Adaptation to Imposed Demands) principle states that the body will adapt to the demand.[4] For example, if you desire to lose or gain weight, the body must respond to an increase or decrease of a certain element like water intake, volume of activity, volume for food intake. If you want to increase your savings account, you have to place a specific demand on the amount of money being spent. The specificity of the demand is vital to this process, if you are planning to be a world-class sprinter, incorporating training activities that include high mileage can severely hinder your progress.

The SAID principle is just as applicable in our thought lives. GOATs understand that mental training is important. If you have goals to accomplish, your thoughts must line up. GOATs only consider the extreme outcome, being the best. Therefore, the words you speak and the ones you take in, help to shape your outcome. If your environment is negative, then you have to turn up the volume on the positive influences. As you challenge or impose a demand upon yourself, you will adapt accordingly in any area.

"The more you do something, the more likely it is that you will do it again in the future. Repetition rewires the brain and breeds habits. The more the neurons fire together, the more likely it is that they will fire together in the future." - John Arden[6]

The elite athlete seeking to become the best, must exert the best effort in each area of training. This is not to be confused with pursuing perfection. No one is perfect, but we can make every attempt to be our best selves, every time. By maximizing each rep, each interval, each task, these GOATs or GOATs-in-waiting are able to recruit every tool and resource designed for their success.

Two quotes come to mind:

"Go hard or go home..." - Unknown

and

"Everything we could ever need for
life and godliness has already been
deposited in us by His divine power.
2 Peter 1:3-4 The Passion Translation[7]

Whatever you are designed to do, you already
have it. Tapping into it is the most important
thing and with the proper training, it has the
ability to be fully realized. This is true in
not only sports but can be applied to all that
we do.

BALANCE AND COORDINATION

In many parts of the world, the elite athlete is the
epitome of strength and success. This image is just
that, an image. People may see these athletes with
innate talent and may miss the hard work, mistakes, or
pitfalls along the way. By seeing only their strengths,

we characterize them by those strengths, and therefore dehumanize them. Life is about balance. Yin and yang, ebb and flow, up and down.

"Any strength overplayed can become a weakness" - Unknown

The core is the key to finding that balance. Once that balance is established then coordination of all other movements is possible. For the athlete, the core is a group of muscles that work synergistically to stabilize the body, so that when movement is required it has a solid base. In life, it is that internal core: the mind, body, and spirit that must be in balance. Without it the ability to focus and achieve your goals can be derailed.

ENDURANCE

NO quitters allowed. Endurance is the ability to maintain and work through something over time.[8] Being balanced and being able to stabilize through in a stationary position is easy without an enormous amount of effort. For a person standing still looking in the mirror, it would be relatively easy to pick up your foot. However, when movements such as swinging your entire leg from front to back are incorporated, the task becomes more challenging. Endurance underscores this dynamic component of training.

Doing something new or challenging for the first time is often difficult. If we focus on that one occurrence and how it made us feel it could deter us from ever doing it again. I use a therapeutic muscle recovery technique with my clients that initially might be uncomfortable. It may even elicit occasional complaints of pain. However, as soon as we are done, they report nothing but positive results that include a better range of motion, increased power, and improved functional movement. Wouldn't you know it, they make sure that I include it as part of the treatment plan at the next office visit. Over time, these clients have come to endure and trust the process that results in growth, development strength, and power.

SPEED, POWER AND EFFICIENCY

Speed is described as the rate at which a task or a movement is performed.[9] While efficiency is the measure of effectiveness in the performance of that movement. In other words, speed is how fast you do something and efficiency deals with the quality at which you do it. Most sports have a time component to them. Running is a sport that is defined by one's ability to go from one point to another over time. The winner is the one who achieves their goal, the finish line, over a given amount of time.

Power is the generation of force or strength over time.[4] It is evident in the push out of the starting blocks, the elevation of the high jumper, or even a football lineman's block.

When training it is important to focus on the end from the beginning. On the way to becoming a GOAT, there will be several opportunities to repeat tasks.

With each rep, the focus on quality is vital and will lead to not only better performance but an increase in speed. GOATs work hard and do so with intention and excellence.

FLEXIBILITY

Being flexible is more than being able to stretch. In sports, it is the ability to maximize the range of motion at a particular joint. The proper level of flexibility helps to facilitate movement, correct muscular and postural imbalances, enhance power generation and, to reduce likelihood of injury to the elite athlete.[4]

Life too, can be more enjoyable with an approach that is relatively flexible. Organization and systems are important, but being too rigid can contribute to distress and delays. You can plan and plan and plan, but if you have no room when an "audible" is called, then frustration can set in.

The COVID-19 pandemic is a case in point. The world suddenly seemed to come to a halt. With respect to the sports industry and every industry for that matter, adaptability was the key to maintaining any sort of operation. The ability to adapt to the changing health and safety recommendations and regulations allowed teams and individuals to train and compete at a high level.

Being flexible does not mean that you have to give up your goals, you just have to be willing to be open to the process of looking different.

QUEST TO REFLECT:

- Is there an area of your life that is out of balance?

- How does that imbalance impact other people?

- In what ways have you tried to find that balance?

CHAPTER 3:

In the Blocks

You have set your eyes on the goal. You have trained for months or maybe years for this day. Your nutrition, sleep and training routines have been flawless. You are completely "locked in".

FIRST CALL....bib numbers pinned...

SECOND CALL...spikes on and laces tied

FINAL CALL...

All checked in, you are escorted to the starting line.

ZONE ONE...Clear

ZONE TWO...Clear

ZONE THREE...Clear

ZONE FOUR...Clear

RUNNERS, TAKE YOUR MARKS!

You back your legs into the blocks.

SET!!!

You are frozen. Heart racing. Breathing controlled. Each spike wrapped foot, pressed into the pedals, set with intention. Your blood-drained fingertips forced into the rough, almost prickly track hold you in angular position. Like a loaded cannon, you are poised, full of potential, full of dreams, full of hope, full of power waiting to be realized. The starter pistol in the air is prepared to release the field of competitors, and then you.......

WAIT!!!

What about all that I had done correctly to get to this moment? I am ready!! What are we waiting for? If I am ready, shouldn't we all be ready? RIGHT? How long do we have to stay in this position? Why don't they just start? Who is moving? If they aren't ready, then that's on them. That means that I have a better chance of standing out.

How many times have you practiced, studied, prepared for a moment only to WAIT?

Who wants to wait? What does waiting patiently accomplish?

Patience is described as the ability or willingness to suppress restlessness or annoyance when confronted with delay.[10] Patience requires character, fortitude, and stability. If you don't rely on these as your default, life has a way of giving do-overs by putting you into situations that will test your patience.[11]

Baseball and football are very
different games. In a way, both
of them are easy. Baseball is
easy if you've got patience,
and football is easy if you
understand patience. - Bo
Jackson, NFL and MLB Hall of
Famer

Sometimes you may feel as if you have all the
right credentials, the right connections, you are in the
right place and you have to wait. How you wait is the
key. There are people watching you. People are
watching to see how you react under pressure. Will
you be poised? Will you be diligent? Will you display
self-control? Will you be optimistic? Will you throw a
tantrum to get your way? Road rage anyone?

1:30 P.M...I lie there
partially disrobed, strapped to
a radiation treatment table.

WAITING. Controlling every breath so as to not move my head, neck or chest.

THINKING. Will this burn me? Will it make me worse? No, I am already healed. They took it all out. I know I saw it. How long will this take? My nose itches, CRAP!! I have a meeting when I get back to the office. I have to sneeze, I have to sneeze. SHIT! My bad, I am listening to Jesus music. Focus...When can I get up? I have stuff to do. I feel like I have been here for an hour, right? Ok now I have to pee. Are you kidding me? ZZZZZ, wait...did I just fall asleep?

Please hurry... Finally!!!

Thank you, God! 1:35 P.M.

When we are willing to wait to see our goal be realized, it could potentially be the most difficult process. It may seem lonely and isolated. You may have to remind yourself of the goal at hand. You may have to re-evaluate your circle of influence. You may have to visualize all of the work that it took to get to his moment. But when you are in the proper position, patiently waiting and open to being the fullest expression of all that you contain, it is the perfect opportunity for your purpose to be revealed.

How do you know when your purpose is being revealed? Purpose is not going to show up on a designated day.[12] It doesn't show up just because you are tired of doing something else. Your purpose is made obvious when you are at peace. It is the thing that brings you to a place of peace.

Peace is an ancient term that has several connotations. During biblical times the Hebrew derivation of the word referred to the state of wholeness, with nothing missing.[13] Other versions of peace describe a state of tranquility or absence of turmoil or happiness. It also refers to a sense of agreement, covenant, or connection. As we look at our goals and the journey toward them, each interpretation of the word peace requires a look internally. It involves an internal assessment.

Am I in position?

Have I walked in patience? Did I slow down enough to hear what I need to hear or see what I need to see?

Am I connecting with what I am doing at this moment? Does this bring me happiness? Is it moving me to connect to a need or problem that I can help to solve?

If the answer is yes, then your purpose is being revealed to you.

It may not come all at once but if you are intentional about finding your purpose, it will definitely find you.

- POSITION
- PATIENCE
- PEACE
- PURPOSE
- POWER

CHAPTER 4:

Staying in Your Own Lane

POW!!!

And they (you) are off!!!

On the way to achieving your goal, you may find that the reason you are pursuing it may be challenged. But your purpose is just that, your purpose.

Purpose is a dynamic concept. It is not always concrete. It evolves and grows. Your purpose is often something that requires more than you can do on your own. It can make you uncomfortable and force you to expand your thoughts, your vision, your circle, or even your heart.

How do you know what your purpose is?

Purpose is the reason for the creation or the reason for a certain action being performed. Goals are derivatives of our thoughts and dreams. What we dream or spend time thinking about is linked to our purpose. No one can change your purpose. It is divinely imparted. It is the basis on which you are built. Your height, your skin, your ethnicity, your shape all play a role in the full expression of your purpose. Your place of origin or even the family to whom you were born to contribute to your ultimate purpose. Successes and failures each help lead you to the things that you were created to do. And they will both surely be a part of your story.

- What drives you?
- What drives you crazy?
- Is there a problem that needs you to solve?
- Is there something that keeps you up at night?

- What would you do or what skill do you have that brings joy to others?

- What would you do if you never received money for it?

- Who relies on you?

- Have you succeeded at something consistently?

- In what areas have you failed?

While this list of questions is not comprehensive, it does give some insight regarding your purpose. Just because you find your purpose, does not mean that it will guarantee that you achieve your goals. However, by understanding and remembering your goals, you will stay on track in the pursuit of them.

As an athletic trainer, I have always had plans to work at the highest levels of the industry. To most people that means working in professional sports. I can truly say that I have been blessed to enjoy a career of over twenty years in athletic training in a variety of settings. From youth sports to entrepreneurship, high school sports to professional sports, outpatient clinical to education and advocacy, I have been pretty busy. Along the way, I found that I enjoyed certain aspects of each setting more than others, but I never lost my affinity for my craft.

I knew that I chose this profession because it combined my love of sports and my background in science. It has allowed me to do things that I enjoy and get paid for it. But it didn't give me my purpose. I found my purpose when I was doing things that weren't a true job requirement. My career has given me a platform.

Along the path to your goals, distractions may come. Looking around at your peers and comparing your differences in progress can cause devastating consequences. Imagine the gun going off, you are racing down the track, you may even be in the lead but you see another runner in the corner of your eye. Then suddenly, you begin to drift. Drifting right into the next lane, not much but just enough to move out of your purpose. All of the work and preparation that you have done to get to this point, only to leave you disqualified. This can happen to anyone. I have even found myself in this situation more than once.

Occasionally, I have gotten off track when I have followed what others have said about what I would be good at, without checking it against my "purpose compass", my peace. When I have pursued a project, an activity, or even a relationship (professional or personal) and peace is not present, it never goes well. I find myself forgetting what my goals were and wasting time following that which may not align with my values and ultimately my purpose.[14]

Race horses are outfitted to prevent these deviations. The blinders that they wear around their eyes are designed to facilitate better focus, alignment, or pull on the track, increased speed, and reduce stress. We should take notes from the race horse and put on our own blinders. We must protect ourselves from negative words, competing with someone who is not our competition, and excessive busyness.

This is the case with GOATs, the gift, talent, or occupation that may have been what got them recognized or where success was realized, may just be the vehicle to discovering their true purpose. Allyson Felix is the most decorated track and field athlete in the world.[15] Her athleticism and excellence on the track got our attention. However, her work and advocacy off the track has sparked changes in how corporations work with women. She has used her platform to push for policy changes in maternal health care for black women and promotes education initiatives around the world. What some people think is their purpose, may not even scratch the surface.

QUEST TO REFLECT:

- Have you ever felt like you had no direction or guidance for your choices?

- If so, on what did you base your decision-making?

- How do you limit distractions as you are pursuing a goal?

CHAPTER 5:

Getting over the hurdles

So you have discovered your purpose. Suited up, shoes laced, you are in the proper position, you are "locked-in" and focused on the finish line. You are ready to run YOUR race.

Guns up, and you're off. Running. Running. Running. "Uh oh, what is that in front of me? Hurdle? No way. No one said anything about hurdles."

Hurdles are fine if you know they are there. Then you have trained for years to hurdle, your body knows what to expect. It knows the number of steps from the blocks to the first hurdles. The speed needed to get over it is a second thought, you have prepared for obstacles. The alternating legs and arms that power through are almost on auto-pilot. Perfectly timed hurdles spaced evenly, each obstacle is unalarming and predictable.

"But I am not a hurdler. I am ready for a different race. How do I get over it? I don't want to fall. If I fall, I might fail. Can I quit and start over?"

I am convinced that at some point we have all felt stuck in the middle of a journey only to hit an obstacle without warning. How we get beyond those obstacles is the key to success. Sometimes these roadblocks may seem impossible to get past. Job losses, natural disasters, relationship drama, discrimination, or literal hurdles can cause a variety of responses. Anxiety, stress, loss of focus, physical changes, and potentially poor decision making can be a result.

I have spent more than 20 years in Houston, TX. My career in sports medicine led me here and has guided my decision to stay and establish roots. I have enjoyed my time but it has not been absent of challenges. It often seemed like every time I got settled or on a trajectory, a hurdle was inevitable. After a few years, I was married with kids and planning for a lifetime together and suddenly all of that changed. I started over with hopes of building my business, buying a house and having a happy healthy family. Then, here comes a hurricane and an economic recession. I got a new job and I loved it, but when I lost a student it lost its shine. I chose to focus on family and go back to school. I always want to be the best at anything that I pursue. Making good progress, I was moving along, working a simpler schedule raising my children, and then suddenly I got a diagnosis following a simple sinus procedure. Facing what the doctors felt was a potential death sentence, I had yet another hurdle to attack. Made it through that one, got a promotion that would take my career and family to the next level, settled into this dream house, and then...another hurricane. We packed up, moved out, and hopped from hotel to hotel. I found myself extremely stressed out and exhausted.

Looking for solutions and next steps, I reflected on my training as a former hurdler, I understand that pursuing goals can be hard work. I know what it is like to be on track and something pops up in front of you. It can throw you off balance even if you know it is coming your way. Occasionally, a hurdle may have been placed in the wrong position forcing me to change my routine and the number of steps between that one and the next. I remember a track meet during college, it actually happened to me. It required focus, composure, and determination. All of the training and conditioning kicked in.   I was forced to make adjustments, but remained true to my purpose. I was empowered to attack whatever came my way. I woke up every day to pray and read. I read the same things every day. I declared what God's word said about me. I wrote out affirmations about myself. I protected my space. I watched the words that I spoke out loud. No matter how many times I thought about all the negative outcomes that could be ahead, I refused to give in to them. I got quiet and limited my interactions to lock into my goals. Unyielding, I competed with myself to keep going, even when it was hard.

Power is the ability to cause an action or to exert control, leverage, or authority over situations or entities.[16] Power is gained or lost based on our positioning, levels of patience, peace and ability to connect to our purpose. When you are not in the proper position, you may start off okay, but end up traveling outside of your lane. When you are lacking patience or peace, your response to life's challenges could be premature and driven by emotions. It could lead to errors or even regret. When you are operating out of your purpose, you could even find yourself off the track or and out of the race altogether. Power is the strength you tap into when you fight to stay or to get back on track.

What happens if we just avoid the hurdles or go around them?

You lose your power. Life has a way of forcing us to learn lessons. When we avoid challenges or difficulties, we detrain or lose the ability to grow and develop in every area of our lives. Just as we discussed the SAID Principle in Chapter 2, the same concept is in effect when we experience these challenges. We have to do the work and succeed at going beyond our perceived limitations. When we avoid it, we miss the lesson and are doomed to repeat the process of learning the lesson. We can find ourselves powerless by letting life happen to us instead of being able to move forward and be empowered to attack whatever comes to threaten the achievement of our goals.

While my life experiences may seem like I had a pretty tough run, I can now look back and only see victory after victory. The power that I found came from a place much bigger than myself. Some call it the universe or the creator, intuition, but I call Him, God. My connection is deep and gives me the reassurance that no matter what struggles, challenges or hurdles I may encounter that I am not alone. I know that I will make it past them and somehow end up stranger than I was before. It is the SAID Principle. I am resilient, made stronger through each hurdle, enabled to attack because I know my purpose and it is POWERED by God.

QUEST TO REFLECT:

What do you believe is your PURPOSE?

- From where do you draw your strength, your POWER?

- Give an example of a situation when you were able to attack a hurdle that life handed you.

- How did you conquer it?

CHAPTER 6:

Recovery Plan - Getting back to your lane and purpose

You have made it through to the finish line, your goal. Some of you may have done it kicking, screaming, crawling, or even being dragged across the line. But you have surely made it through.

> "Anything worth having is worth fighting for?" - Andrew Carnegie

On the way to your goals, you may feel as if you have engaged in a full-on battle. A battle is a struggle to beat or achieve something.[17] It can be described as an encounter with the opposition during the course of an even greater war.

Battles are ugly. While strategic in structure and formation, battles leave painful reminders of their wake. When countries go to war, the smaller battles leave a trail of ammunition, destroyed homes, businesses, places of worship, and people injured or dead, both combatants and civilians.

Sports are similar to war. They represent a series of battles, called matches, games, meets, tournaments. It is an opportunity to pursue a goal through encounters with obstacles in the form of competitors. Some battles are won, others are left wanting in defeat. Victory for some is in the conquering and for others, it is merely survival.

You may be wounded, but your mere existence is proof that there is more work to do. There is more to overcome, more to build, more to celebrate. Wounds are proof of life and the scars they leave are proof of recovery.[18]   Following any contest or battle, must come a reset.

REFUEL

Fuel is an essential part of any pursuit or undertaking. When we are striving toward something, fatigue can set in. We are subject to depleting our nutrients and the energy that empowers us to move or even mentally process. It is important to replenish what you have lost, but you must be intentional. The proper balance of electrolytes and fluids helps to rehydrate the tissues. Carbohydrates are sources of quick energy sources and can be stored in the muscles and the liver. Fats are used to insulate, assist with temperature regulation, nerve conduction, and storage. While proteins are primary repair agents and building blocks of cells and tissue. The human body needs all of these to not only perform, but to survive. In refueling, all of the nutrients and minerals must be included.[15]

Just as in replenishment following a competition, we have to put back the things we may have lost in the battle toward our goals. Along the way, it is not uncommon to lose hope. Hope is the expectation or anticipation of something happening. This can be tempting when you are waiting for the realization of your goal. We might also lose focus. Battle fatigue can cause you to lose sight of the goal. Refueling gives you the energy to think more clearly. When you revisit your purpose and reconnect with the people and environments that remind you of who you are, your vision can once again become clear.

A huge part of my business has been staging, staffing, and managing sports-related events. I find myself running around, answering questions, treating injuries, delegating tasks, and making other people look their best. I love it! I enjoy the adrenaline rush and the satisfaction of being a part of something bigger than myself. No matter how energized I am during the events, I am often left depleted. This is a place of crossroads and I find that I can choose to refill or to continue to run until only fumes remain, physically, mentally, and emotionally. I refuel by doing the little things: going to the nail shop, grabbing a good meal that I didn't cook, and a nap with no alarm clock. It goes a long way and the next thing you know, I am back "on my grind."

REST

Rest is arguably the most important component to recovery. I encourage my athletes to develop a good sleep routine. Sleeping is a common method. However, it is not the only one. Getting the proper amounts of rest can include other activities like yoga, finding a quiet place, reading a book, taking a walk, meditation, or even journaling. The key is to take a break from your normal level of work or activity. It downshifts the intensity of your energy, recycling it and allowing it to be refreshed for the next time you need it. Rest is a stress reliever and reduces anxiety. It helps to boost your mood, your metabolism, alleviate pain and improve healing. When you continue to run and run without a reprieve, not only can the immune system but all of the body's organ systems can be compromised.[18]

" In order to go fast, you have to be able to slow down" - Dr. Erin Hassler

No, we are not machines; no matter how much we push ourselves or allow ourselves to be pushed. Mind over matter thinking can only go so far. By slowing down, even for a small stint, we can take in the work that we have already done. We can appreciate the progress we have made and get a fresh vision for the future.

I think of the COVID-19 pandemic and the new found appreciation for the rest that people throughout the world experienced. Unfortunately, despite the devastating losses of friends and loved ones, it was also a time of rest and renewal. The trees, the soil, the bodies of water were still. The animals were able to experience less harsh environments. Many of us were able to have altered work schedules, virtual options and some were just off work. In the midst of layoffs and furloughs, the opportunity to pause was made more available.

The fruit of this respite resulted in new ways of doing work, new businesses, new careers, a new appreciation for relationships, more creative expressions of the gifts and talents of individuals. We saw humanity unify in the face of racism, fear, and hatred. Rest from being overscheduled, overworked, and underappreciated made many of us more sensitive to the needs of other people and our own. It is my hope that we can all rest more intentionally and not wait for the next global crisis to force it.

REHAB

On the way to your goals, there may be some nagging, lingering aches, or pains. Sometimes that last battle may have felt like the last stand and that you won't bounce back. If you are still here, then there is still work to be done. Our lives and dreams and hopes can use a little tune-up on the way to becoming the GOAT

Rehabilitation is the process of restoring to a previous state, to health, or to normalcy, by way of therapy and training.[5] There are steps to coming back from a tough place, an injury, a layoff, a divorce, a miscarriage, addiction...loss. As you are reloading and exercising those weak spots, it is important to protect yourself and to be well balanced. Braces, crutches, or limitations to the amount of work you can do are ways to keep you from more damage. Stability is a necessary component of any rehab program. It is vital that you are on a firm surface to prevent you from falling. So remember your purpose, it will give you the solid ground you need to put in work.

The next step in getting back on track is to restore the range of motion. In sports medicine, that refers to the amount of movement available at a given joint. It is important that movement be unrestricted in order to generate the force needed to bear the load. In rehabilitating our goals and dreams, we have to move. Remaining stagnant and allowing fear, frustration, discouragement to creep in, lock up the joint, and the ability to handle the hard things that life brings. Life can guarantee one thing, for sure; nothing ever stays the same. Being able to adjust or adapt to changes contributes to the strength development required for promotion in every aspect of your life.[5]

Restoring strength and power is a pivotal step and it has the most dynamic characteristics. Iso-this, iso-that, concentric, eccentric, there are so many different approaches to muscular development. There are free weights, machine weights, multi-directional multiplanar exercises. Bodyweight, bands, tubes, plyometric exercises all enable us to not only bear weight, but to generate force. It helps us fight back. It helps us withstand and it is systematic. How we train in a given area will translate into fortitude, strength, and power in the direction that it is intended. Remember that the SAID Principle states that when we place demands on a specific tissue or in a specific area, the tissue or area will respond.[5] And isn't that the goal, to get the outcome we desire? When we demand that our environment is positive, when we put in our reps, when we keep telling ourselves who we truly are, we are building that strength. We are being restored. It is the place of peace, not perfection but POWER.

CHAPTER 7:

GOAT Squad – If you are the smartest person in the room, you need a bigger room and circle.

So you have done it! You have accomplished your goal or maybe even a few of them. It was probably not without a few obstacles along the way. Challenges are designed to position you for advancement. Resistance is the key component in the SAID Principle. A theory built on the concept that in order to build, grow or advance overloading is a necessity.

Life without resistance is the clear path to death. - Dr. Erin Hassler

We all have a path to follow, and it will take the direction designed just for you. Our dreams and goals are used to light that journey, but it is your purpose that is the true compass.

Becoming the GOAT is not about arriving. It is about living, experiencing, learning, teaching, loving, forgiving, and giving back. In life, all of these actions are fluid and continuous. When fully expressed, they are not finite and have no shelf-life. They can go on until your final breath.

GREATEST OF ALL TIME

GOATs are:

- hardworking
- risk-takers
- focused
- self-disciplined
- adaptable
- intentional
- passionate

- authentic

- intuitive

- influential

- sacrificing

- grateful

Being the GOAT is about leaving things better than you found them. It is about being a leader. GOATs are thermostats and not thermometers. They change every room that they enter and encourage others to do the same. GOATs are impassioned and contagious. They are muses for our dreams.

GOATs are daring and think far beyond the boundaries of any box. Limits are the starting line and every accomplished goal is just another opportunity to measure growth. They are willing to fail, so they can go even higher the next time. GOATs are dynamic and they reinvent themselves. Stagnation is the antithesis. GOATs don't just follow rules, they create them.

Sacrifice is second nature for GOATs.. Sacrifice is giving up something of value: time, money, experience, resources, encouragement, knowledge. They understand that in order to gain, they have to first give. Gratefulness is what sets GOATs apart. They understand that they did not accomplish anything without the help of others. GOATs are committed to being the best version of themselves and putting in the work to do it.

GOATs are janitors, teachers, doctors, lawyers, students, plumbers, welders, doctors, plant operators, cooks, daycare workers, make-up artists, hair stylists, engineers, accountants, preachers, believers, coaches, advocates, administrators, analysts, artists, designers, content creators, podcasters, musicians, athletes, athletic trainers, developers, gamers, parents, grandparents, aunties, uncles, siblings, linesisters, friends, mentors, counselors, experts, and so much more. The real GOAT is YOU!

CHAPTER 8:

GOAT to I.M.P.A.C.T.!

So you're the GOAT, now what's next? What do you do when you have become the BEST YOU? Well, the answer is, you use your status to make an IMPACT. We were all created to make a difference in the lives of others. We are each connected to one another. Some of the most recognizable public figures deemed to be GOATs have made more of an impact away from their sport or area of expertise.

IMPACT

- *The action of one object coming forcibly into contact with another; a collision*
- *Come into forcible contact with another object; Have a strong effect on someone or something*

*-   The force of impression of one thing on another;
     a significant or major effect[19]*

Danny Thomas, an American entertainer had a goal: to be successful enough as an entertainer to provide for his family. Well, he achieved that and surpassed it. He worked as a comedian, musician, producer and even acted in his own television show. With a career spanning decades, he even dabbled in business and was the first minority owner of the Miami Dolphins, a team in the National Football League.[20]

However, it is the work that Thomas championed through the St. Jude Children's Research Hospital in Memphis, TN that has left the biggest legacy. Together with his wife and now his daughter, the hospital has provided care, treatment, and support services for children with cancer and their families, at no charge. Known worldwide for their impact in the healthcare industry, St. Jude has committed that they "won't stop until no child dies from cancer." Now that is real IMPACT. The gifts that made Danny Thomas famous made room for his impact.[21]

Someone or something impacted or inspired him to give back to fight for other people. Have you been impacted, influenced, or inspired to do something? Have you been able to do the same for someone else?

INTEGRITY

- *firm adherence to a code of especially moral or artistic values: INCORRUPTIBILITY*
- *an unimpaired condition: SOUNDNESS*
- *the quality or state of being complete or undivided: COMPLETENESS*[22]

When people have integrity, it can be best seen in their sense of right and wrong. We all have a general understanding of morality. But to have integrity, a person will do the right thing when no one else is around. There is a quote by George Berkeley that asks, "if a tree falls in the forest and no one is around to hear it, does it make a sound?"[23]

Of course, it does. We have all done something, even unintentionally when there were no witnesses. We might have even thought we had gotten away with it. Then wouldn't you know it, there were consequences of that decision or action. No matter what kind of isolation or vacuum in which it occurred, it still happened.

With a science exam approaching, TJ had spent most of his time after school on video games and watching videos on social media. Test day arrived and he slept 40 of the 50 minutes allotted, only answering 8 of the 50 questions. A few days later the teacher returned the graded exams and TJ scored 95%. Integrity would dictate that TJ inform the teacher in case of any error or oversight.

Now the real question is what would you do if you were TJ?

MOTIVES

- *need or desire that causes a person to act*
- *underlying cause to action*
- *a force, stimulus or influence:*
  INCENTIVE/DRIVE[24]

Motives are not necessarily the same as motivation. It is the motive that is the pure/root reason for making a choice or taking an action. Motivation is what drives or pushes one to do something.[25] The motives can occasionally have a negative tone, but it can also be applied in a positive way.

Employment is a real factor in the health of not only local and global economies but in the lives of individuals. It can help someone find purpose or even options that they didn't know they had. Well, how you present yourself in the job search process can be a gamechanger. Being intentional in your resume layout, online profile or even your interview attire are all examples of having a positive motive.

PASSION

-       *a feeling of strong or constant regard for and dedication to someone or something*

-       *devotion, preference, appetite, allegiance, desire*[26]

GOATs often find recognition, fame, acknowledgment or success in a certain sport, industry, or field of study. However, the most significant impact they make in this world has occurred when they follow their passions. Their commitment to a cause or a purpose that affects a country, community, or a specific initiative, might be their greatest legacy.

Olympic gold medalist and prize-fighting boxer, Muhammed Ali was known for his athleticism and strategy. However, his crowning achievement was his activism against racial injustice in the United States.[27] He was so passionate about his position that he joined the Nation of Islam, a religious organization.[28] Ali was even criminally convicted, though later exonerated, for refusing induction into the Army - citing religious objections. Ali went on the fight again and earned the world heavyweight title. He worked tirelessly to bring visibility to injustice and went on to receive the Presidential Medal of Freedom in 2005.

Regardless of your political affiliation, personal opinion on racial interactions, or accuracy of the history of this country, there is at least one person that can be credited with starting the conversation about race in the United States. As with Ali at the height of his protests, Colin Kapernick made lots of enemies in his attempt to bring awareness to something close to his heart. As the quarterback of the NFL's San Francisco 49ers, he united fans. As an activist, his actions sparked division but it made us talk and talk and talk. He will forever be known more for what he did off the field, rather than as a football player.

After over 20 years in the sports medicine and education industries, I have enjoyed success in what has been an often difficult system to crack. I thought that my passion was for the craft, for the healing arts, and teaching.

But one day I met a young lady, JS. A bright and energetic student aide, who wanted to have a career in athletic training. She was a senior in high school but much younger than her peers. However, it seemed as if JS was far more mature than them as well. She was an excellent student, an athlete, made time to care for her siblings, and even worked. I saw something in her that reminded me of myself.

Self-motivated with confidence to match, JS was known for coming into the athletic training room and taking charge, even if I were standing right there. She had a way of lighting up any room. I could trust her to "be me". I was elated when we got her into a college athletic training program. We talked about how we would work together once she finished.

One Friday, JS called me to catch me up on things. We talked about school, relationships, family, and the future. We spoke regularly but this call was different. She said, "I want to be just like you." I was proud and excited at the same time. The call ended with an "I love you" and "talk to you later. Two days later, she was gone.

The hole that this loss left was big. It hurt. Everything that she wanted to do on this earth would go unfulfilled. It was hard to talk to her family, I didn't want to be a reminder of loss. I knew that I had to do something. I promised to do "something" in her name.

She was my "little sister" and I wanted to make sure that she would be remembered.

A few years later, I found myself in a new job. Vowing never to allow myself to be that close again, I kept my head down and worked harder than ever. My focus was on my family and staying healthy. Then, it found me. My passion! All of the things that I learned about the industry, business, leadership had to be passed on. All of the things that I would share with JS but couldn't. Mentorship would be at the heart of my IMPACT. And I take her with me everywhere that I go! I want to make sure that I impact as many people as I can, the way that she impacted me.

AUTHENTICITY

To be authentic is to believe that something is based on fact or is original.[29] Being authentic is about being genuine, pure and honest. Realizing your GOAT status requires hard work and dedication. It also comes with an enormous amount of growth and development.

Physical growth is inevitable in the athlete, but it is the internal growth that requires an honest look into who you really are. That can be a massive undertaking. It is necessary to be "real" with yourself when you do. It is important to understand what makes you happy, sad, angry, satisfied, or discontent.

Making excuses and justifying decisions, whether good or bad, can have a way of stifling authenticity. It is nearly impossible to see the real you with blinders on. Otherwise, you will go through the motions and will never work on the real areas of weakness. Real growth occurs when you are really real. This process can be extremely uncomfortable and painful. Occasionally you may feel isolated, but it is worth it because it always leads to truth.

COMPASSION

Compassion is the combination of awareness and desire to alleviate the distress or misfortune of others.[30] Legacies are made from the IMPACT you

leave on people and the world. Impact occurs when

there is a genuine consideration of the needs of others.

Compassion is characterized in little acts of

kindness toward people who may be suffering,

struggling or with an unmet need. In the world of

sports, it is the awareness of a coach to know that

today might be the day to ease off, in the midst of an

athlete's personal crisis.

Compassion is the use of one's platform to

change the trajectory of someone else's course for the

better. I am immediately reminded of professional

basketball player Maya Moore.[31] Statistically, she is

the winningest collegiate basketball player. She is a

multi-year WNBA Champion, WNBA All-Star, and

honored as 2017 Performer of the Year.[32] At the height

of her athletic career, Maya stepped off the court to

push for criminal justice reform. "Win with Justice" is

the movement she initiated to educate the public on how the judicial system works.

Honored with 2021 ESPY The Arthur Ashe Award for Courage, Maya clearly understood and expressed how her GOAT status is supposed to be used.[33]

"Power is not meant to be
gripped with a clenched fist,
...[it] is meant to be handled
generously so we can
thoughtfully empower one
another to thrive in our
communities, ...championing
our humanity before our
ambitions." - Maya Moore

TENACITY (PERSEVERANCE)

-       *continued effort to do or achieve something*
despite difficulties, failure or opposition: the action or
condition or an instance or persevering:
STEADFASTNESS[34]

-       *persistence, purposefulness, resolve, confidence,*
fortitude
-the quality that allows someone to continue trying to
do something even though it is difficult[35]

One characteristic that seems to continuously
show up in GOATs is perseverance. They don't
understand what it means to quit or give up. No matter
the challenge, it is the ability to "push through" and
persist that separates the GOAT from the rest of the
pack. In the world of sports, there are so many
examples of athletes who persevered despite the odds
of winning or sometimes even completing the
competition.

Michael Jordan was not always a world champion. He had a very ordinary start to an extraordinary on-court career. Determined to be the best, he worked on his craft every chance he got. He studied and continued to challenge himself. He was his own greatest competitor, resulting in multiple NBA championships, titles, and accolades and even spending a short time as a professional baseball player and actor. Since retirement, Jordan has carved out a name for himself as a businessman, including major ownership in the NBA's Charlotte Hornets franchise and his own NASCAR racing team. Now, he is providing opportunities for others to be employed and perhaps follow their own dreams.

In writing this book, I spent time considering the stories of so many people who I admire and to whom I look up. But when I go back through my own timeline,

I am actually surprised. Mine is a story of nothing but perseverance.

A once insecure and awkward "tomboy", occasionally left out of the popular crowd, I am now a healthy and happy adult. And I am completely grateful for every challenge and opportunity to grow. Growth is not always an enjoyable process but it is necessary to the fulfillment of one's purpose.

Growth for me was persevering to get into an industry that did not roll out the red carpet for women. It was this same persistence that made me apply to every NBA, NFL, WNBA, and MLB team for any kind of opportunity to work in my field. It was still perseverance when I held on to each rejection letter as visual reminders that one day, I would work as an athletic trainer in professional sports. They weren't NOs to me, they were whispers of YESs.

It was also perseverance when just a few years into a struggling marriage with three young kids that I wanted so badly to make it work, I kept going, kept praying, kept loving and forgiving. Many people think that GOATs are successful because things just seem to fall into place for them. They make it look easy, but success comes as a result of prevailing in the midst of challenges.

Tenacity is the resulting quality that develops every time you don't give up. Tenacity increases every time you fight through a different situation. Battle-by-battle, hurdle-by-hurdle, hater-by-hater, not only do your physical muscles get stronger, so do your mental and emotional ones. You recover more quickly. Being tenacious enables you to move more easily through new challenges, and just know that there will always be new challenges.

QUEST TO REFLECT:

- Do you have any goals that seem too big to accomplish?

- What has happened when you limited your own efforts or potential to the level of the expectations of others?

- Describe how you would see yourself if you had no limitations?

EPILOGUE

GOATs are people without limitations. There is no struggle that can keep a GOAT from pursuing what they believe is their true purpose. GOATs don't allow disappointments to cause them to give up. This book was written to remind you that being a GOAT is not for celebrities or the elite athlete. If you can find your way to living an authentic existence that hinges on personal development, accountability, and a desire to make a difference in the world around you, then you are on your way to becoming the GOAT, the Greatest (You) of All Time.

-Much Love,

ACKNOWLEDGEMENT

Thanks GP for saying to me [at one of the lowest
points], *"B&#@!, get a job!!"*

Your words have resonated with my desire to live the
life that I deserve. Thanks for the kick in the pants!

Love you,

Linus

ENDNOTES

1. "Goal." *Dictionary.com*, Dictionary.com, www.dictionary.com/browse/goal.

2. "Goal." *Merriam-Webster*, Merriam-Webster, www.merriam-webster.com/dictionary/goal.

3. *Track and Field Coaching Education*, seanbernstein.com/trainingtheory.

4. McGill, Erin, and Ian Montel. *NASM Essentials of Sports Performance Training*. Jones & Bartlett Learning, 2019.

5. Prentice, William E. *Rehabilitation Techniques for Sports Medicine and Athletic Training 6th Ed.* Slack, 2015.

6. Arden, John Boghosian. *Rewire Your Brain: Think Your Way to a Better Life*. Wiley, 2010.

7. "2 Peter 1: NLT Bible: YouVersion." *NLT Bible | YouVersion*, 2021, my.bible.com/bible/116/2PE.1.NLT.

8. "Endurance." *Merriam-Webster*, Merriam-Webster, www.merriam-webster.com/dictionary/endurance.

9. "Speed Synonyms, Speed Antonyms." *Merriam-Webster*, Merriam-Webster, www.merriam-webster.com/thesaurus/speed.

10. "Patience." *Dictionary.com*, Dictionary.com, 2021, www.dictionary.com/browse/patience.

11. "Patience Is a Powerful Mental Tool in Sports: Sports Psychology Today - Sports Psychology." *Sports Psychology Today - Sports Psychology | Provided by Mental Edge Athletics*, 15 Apr. 2011, www.sportpsychologytoday.com/sport-

psychology-for-coaches/patience-is-a-powerfull-mental-tool-in-sports/.

12.   "Purpose." *Dictionary.com*, Dictionary.com, 2021, www.dictionary.com/browse/purpose#:~:text=noun,%3B%20end%3B%20aim%3B%20goal.

13.   "Peace." *The Free Dictionary*, Farlex, 2021, www.thefreedictionary.com/peace.

14.   Henry, Miles. "Why Do Horses Wear Blinders? 4 Primary Reasons." *Horse Racing Sense*, 16 July 2021, horseracingsense.com/why-do-horses-wear-blinders/.

15.   Campoamor, Danielle. "Olympic Star Allyson Felix Speaks out about Traumatic Birth Experience." *TODAY.com*, 22 June 2021, www.today.com/parents/allyson-felix-olympic-star-traumatic-birth-experience-t188436.

16.   "Power." *The Free Dictionary*, Farlex, 2021, www.thefreedictionary.com/power.

17.   "Battle - Dictionary Definition." *Vocabulary.com*, 2021, www.vocabulary.com/dictionary/battle.

18.   "Recovery." *The Free Dictionary*, Farlex, 2021, www.thefreedictionary.com/recovery.

19.   O'Connor, Francis G., et al. *Textbook of Running Medicine.* McGraw-Hill, 2001.

20.   "Impact." *Merriam-Webster*, Merriam-Webster, 2021, www.merriam-webster.com/dictionary/impact.

21.   "Danny Thomas." *IMDb*, IMDb.com, www.imdb.com/name/nm0858683/bio.

22.   "How St. Jude Began." *How St. Jude Began - St. Jude Children's Research Hospital,*

www.stjude.org/about-st-jude/history/how-we-began.html.

23.   "Integrity." *Merriam-Webster*, Merriam-Webster, www.merriam-webster.com/dictionary/integrity.

24.   "A Quote by George Berkeley." *Goodreads*, Goodreads, www.goodreads.com/quotes/334037-if-a-tree-falls-in-a-forest-and-no-one.

25.   "Motive." *Merriam-Webster*, Merriam-Webster, www.merriam-webster.com/dictionary/motive.

26.   "Motivation." *Merriam-Webster*, Merriam-Webster, www.merriam-webster.com/dictionary/motivation.

27.   "Passion Synonyms, Passion Antonyms." *Merriam-Webster*, Merriam-Webster, www.merriam-webster.com/thesaurus/passion.

28. "Muhammad Ali." *Encyclopædia Britannica*, Encyclopædia Britannica, Inc., 30 May 2021, www.britannica.com/biography/Muhammad-Ali-boxer.

29. "Nation of Islam." *Encyclopædia Britannica*, Encyclopædia Britannica, Inc., www.britannica.com/topic/Nation-of-Islam.

30. "Authentic Synonyms, Authentic Antonyms." *Merriam-Webster*, Merriam-Webster, www.merriam-webster.com/thesaurus/authentic.

31. "Compassion." *Merriam-Webster*, Merriam-Webster, 2021, www.merriam-webster.com/dictionary/compassion.

32. Mizoguchi, Karen, and Rachel DeSantis. "Maya Moore Accepts Arthur Ashe Award for Her Work with Criminal Justice Reform at 2021 ESPY Awards." *PEOPLE.com*, 10 July 2021,

people.com/sports/espy-awards-2021-maya-moore-accepts-arthur-ashe-award/.

33.   "About Maya." *Maya Moore*, 2020, mayamoore.com/about/.

34.   Espn. "'Power Is Not Meant to Be Gripped with a Clenched Fist, ... Power Is Meant to Be Handled Generously so We Can Thoughtfully Empower One Another to Thrive in Our Communities, ... Championing Our Humanity before Our Ambitions." -@MooreMaya Pic.twitter.com/NcLo4VdfPh." *Twitter*, Twitter, 11 July 2021, twitter.com/espn/status/1414056724508684291?ref_src=twsrc%5Etfw%7Ctwcamp%5Etweetembed%7Ctwterm%5E1414056724508684291%7Ctwgr%5E%7Ctwcon%5Es1_&ref_url=https%3A%2F%2Fpeople.com%2Fsports%2Fespy-awards-2021-maya-moore-accepts-arthur-ashe-award%2F.

35.   "Tenacity." *Merriam-Webster*, Merriam-Webster, 2021, www.merriam-webster.com/dictionary/tenacity.

36.   "Perseverance." *Merriam-Webster*, Merriam-Webster, 2021, www.merriam-webster.com/dictionary/perseverance.

DR. ERIN HASSLER

A pioneering expert, with over two decades in the sports medicine, management and entertainment industries, Dr. Hassler is a coveted speaker, leader, educator, clinician and proud graduate of Clark Atlanta University and Life University.

She has enjoyed industry success as either a staff or contract Athletic Trainer for several organizations in Texas and abroad.   Dr. Hassler has practiced sports medicine in both public and private school systems, the WNBA, Texas Southern University and the US Olympic Committee. As a volunteer medical provider with USA Track and Field, she has served on international teams, including travel to Canada, South America and Europe and most recently working with the USA team at the 2020 USA Olympic Marathon Trials in Atlanta, Georgia.   As owner of Sportz Factory, she has employed dozens of contractors and student interns. Services provided include event management services and medical coverage for a variety of sporting events and organizations, including AAU Junior Olympics, US Open, NCAA Championship Festivals and a wide variety of youth sports competitions. Through her non-profit activities and philanthropy, she has used her experiences to educate and encourage youth to follow their passions as they prepare for their careers.

In 2018, Hassler earned a Doctor of Athletic Training degree from A.T. Still University, one of the first 50 people in the world to do so. Her enthusiasm for the sports industry has allowed her to frequently lecture on a variety of related topics including leadership, business, career forecasting and sports performance. Influenced by the impact that sports have had in her life, Dr. Erin Hassler strives to make a difference, one athlete at a time.

Made in the USA
Columbia, SC
08 November 2021

48569029R00067